Working Title

CHUCK HARP

Working Title
Copyright © 2020 Chuck Harp
All Rights Reserved
Published by Unsolicited Press
Printed in the United States of America
First Edition Paperback.

No part of this book may be used or reproduced in any manner whatsoever without written permission except in the case of brief quotations embodied in critical articles or reviews.

Unsolicited Press
Portland, Oregon
www.unsolicitedpress.com
orders@unsolicitedpress.com
619-354-8005

Cover Design: Kathryn Gerhardt
Editor: S.R. Stewart
ISBN: 978-1-950730-67-4

to Tom

Poems

The Cheap Seats	8
When the Cymbals Start	9
The Hunt	11
Skills	12
Face to the Firing Squad (The Interview)	13
A Career Move	14
Heard Down the Hall	15
Factory Haiku	16
Taken Toll	17
Loudspeakers	18
Reception	20
Keeping Safe Surroundings	21
Shredder	22
Smoke Break	23
Corporate	24
Between the Hours	25
Pockets	26
Please Hold	28
Born for the Battle	29
Strike	31
Hurry!	33
Breathing Between the Teeth	34
Steady as She Goes	36
Slow Traffic to the Right	37
Cut the Check	39

Steam Whistle	40
Overtime	41
Payday	44
Bodega	45
Working Title	46

Working Title

The Cheap Seats

We're killing the collective
more than
the underside of life.
We cheer for underdogs
as the fat cats with their blood covered claws
snatch food from the plates
of Ma and Pop operations.
Households toeing that line
between the two sides of the tracks
like the fine divide between
reporting the news
and cashing in on a tragedy.
Go dog go!
Just try and keep up
with this savage rat race.
With the flip of a single coin,
you will be searching for change.
Take cover from the crows
that are ready to pick your bones
and leave your family in shambles.
No kibbles and bits;
no piece of the pie.
Cause the pigs insist on hogging everything
from the who cares to the have-nots.

When the Cymbals Start

With a hand to the heavens,
we grab the alarm clock by the throat,
slamming it into the nightstand
over and over and over and over again —
spilling cogs and springs as its organs fail,
and the timepiece bleeds out.
Smashing its face, we leave our mark
in the fragile, spider-webbed, cracked glass.
Its hands sprawled out,
begging for forgiveness
and pleading for mercy,
of which we have none.
Where's our reward?
Where's our breaks
during this high-speed chase?
We get no pit stop.
No halftime to take time.
Like a sewer pipe,
it flows on and on and on.
It reaches out far and wide
until it drops off abruptly.
Not into a bright light at the end
but a dreary scum-soaked cavern.
We wonder on flywheels
and ponder why they spin.
Each morning, we're met
with hollered reminders of struggles,

and each night we fight to counter
the clockwise cycle,
ready to shatter the hourglass,
decapitate the digital,
and dread the dawn of a new day.

The Hunt

Steam lifts from my blue,
chipped mug. It slumbers
silently beside my laptop
as my fingers tap dance
along the fragile, print-stained keys.
Tap. Tap. Tap.
They spew
into the tiny room
of my heat infested studio.
They are still unable to shut out
the *plopping* water droplets that
descend from my busted
rusty kitchen faucet.
It looms over the empty sink.
My eyes inspect
the empty job boards,
relating to my hopes of success
or fixing my shit box
that sits in the driveway
beside the broken souls
that camp outside my building
in tents and blue tarps.
I realize as I scroll along the
white web pages,
I'm one bad day away
from moving in beside them.

Skills

Can you push down your emotions?
Throw everything aside that makes you human?
Can you lose your soul?
Rip the sliver that others may have left?

Can you lie through your teeth
About everything between the walls?
Falsify documents down to the signature?
Get what you want, when you want it?

Can you throw bodies under the bus?
Set and push your friends like dominos?
No emotions? No regrets?
Are you hell in human skin?

Face to the Firing Squad (The Interview)

I feel naked.
My skin is see-through.
For every wall I built –
every façade I constructed –
her dagger sharp eyes peak past it all.

I sit there with my world
displayed on a document,
a billboard to the masses.
Marketing myself as best I can
like I'm a product for sale.
My smile shrieks across the table.
Invest in me!
But still, I sit frostbitten,
cold to all emotion.

She fires questions,
then reloads,
and proceeds to empty another clip.
Shoot to kill as if
my desires were disks blasted out the sky.
Never soaring to new heights
and tearing out feathers
before I could take off to fly.

A Career Move

Ask her what she's got,
and she'll lie, bragging about the good stuff.

Apartment that kisses the clouds,
waiting for her to come home.

A luxury car in the garage,
waiting for her to drive far away.

But she has a dresser for sleeping jewels,
and a TV she can never view.

Friends sitting on the sidelines,
but no family in the game.

Money waiting patiently in the vault
for vacations she'll never take.

Waiting for the sun to rise,
just to burn the midnight oil again.

Heard Down the Hall

They get through with steel tip boots,
beating the floorboards in sync
with fingers tapping against the toolbox.
They mouth secret lyrics
to sooth themselves
as if the words need to come out
or the combined weight will
crush their tongues.
Screwdrivers turn into drumsticks
as the bass from the stereo
bumps off flecks of drywall.

They get by with playlists
and swapped songs, shouting out requests
like drunken karaoke friends who don't
understand last call.
Choruses echo from above
the delicate white ceiling tiles.
All while saws, hammers, and drilling
equipment mix with the
instrumentals to construct
an industrial orchestra from
the job site studio.

Factory Haiku

Peeking out windows
workers imagine fresh air,
free and open winds.

Taken Toll

Lonely sits in a steel box,
hauling change for travelers
who ran for cover over the bridge
after the fun, short weekend.

To the right,
there's only one coworker
left in the line.
The illuminating scanner,
flashing like prize fights,
have taken the place of bulbs
in the ticket taker booths.

She's an island now.
A match in the night.
Just waiting to see
how long it takes
for her light to be snuffed out.

Loudspeakers

Attention customers:
Please do not harm and torture
our already glum group
of customer service slaves.
Life has already done that duty.
Keep your curses to yourself.
The staff does not need that
venom dripping into their ears.
Instead, let that hate fester
into the deepest dark corner
of your tiny Grinch heart.
Let the anger kill you swift and silent
like a friend in the night.

Attention customers:
Please do not destroy our store.
Leave the stock on the shelves,
not scattered on the floor
like innards for vultures.
Stop ripping the guts from macaroni boxes
and cookie sleeves
and candy bags
and bread loaves.
Of course, you can't try every fruit
or rub them against your greasy face.
Don't sip sodas to see if they're too sweet.
You taste it; you buy it.

Attention customers:
As always, remember to act civilized.
Don't throw caution to the wind,
so it flies back in our face.
We work hard for checks and roofs.
For hot meals and warm clothes.
We don't live to serve,
just serve to live.
Let the world be your oyster
but be the pearl inside.

Thank you for shopping with us.

Reception

Hitting the light switch
and opening the gates to her Hell.

Brewing coffee in record time
while dragging her own corpse.

She mimics short speeches
that she heard during her training.

Feeling a need to wrap the phone cord
tight around her voice box.

Threats of firing midmorning
lead to bleeding ears.

Taking abuses like jabs
in the cubical fighting ring.

Tying a smile on her mouth
like the back of a Halloween mask.

Praying for the almighty Mainspring
to hurry around and end the day.

She shuts down at six
to rest her battered soul before tomorrow.

Keeping Safe Surroundings

I'm stuck staring at programs.
Disastrous digits flipping
up and down,
down and up.
Only the framed faces
keep me company
while phones blare out
and towers of papers
pile up towards the sky.
When the colors seep
out from between the lines,
leaving the world gray,
shockingly lifeless, and dull…
With fax machines screeching
death notes to my desires…
I find solace in the knick-knacks
that guard my office space.
Tokens of joy, small toys,
or handmade gifts.
Each one bringing me hope
when the weekend ends
and the workweek begins.

Shredder

The gnawing snarl starts up.
Teeth grind and rip,
slice and shrivel,
taking all privacy and confidentiality
to the wastebasket grave.
Numbers and forms.
IDs and statements.
Fragile lives tossed away
like abandoned children
sentenced to the back alley.

It all seems so appealing.

To disappear completely.
Thoughts of a fresh start.
A new man; a free woman.
Second chances at old dreams
by abandoning all responsibilities.
Flipping the desk on the way out.
The sounds of shredded paper
like the applause in the theater,
calling out to the lowering lights
as the story fades to black.

Nothing like ripping out the reset button.

Smoke Break

Barrel my way downstairs, outside
in the
cold.
Just one quick drag is all I need
or maybe
two.
The fucking morning was as bad
as it
gets.
In through the mouth and out
through the
nose.
Smoke staining my fingers, and hair is
a small
price
to pay for the melting tension that swoons out
in a
puff.
The job, the meeting, and the daily incompetence all leaves
with a
smoke.

Corporate

Far off faces,
as cold as icicle covered tombstones,
turn blind eyes to the slabs of skin
that smack as loud as rubber bottom boots,
marching to the boom of rough hand rhythms.
A man-made evil
lurks over shoulders like a fiend,
pulling strings from the balcony
and watching the puppets dance.
In hands, lie judgement scales,
holding lives and weighing fates.
They stretch, seemingly, for an infinity,
slowing down for the anxious,
speeding up for panic.
Eight-hour judges hand out
hard labor sentences,
ringing bells with its gavel.

Between the Hours

Between the hours,
masks with fake smiles are worn,
hiding emotions from those that wield it like a weapon.

Between the hours,
past decisions pop up behind the eyes,
giving glimpses of futures that come and go.

Between the hours,
peace can be found with memories,
like the fun found with pals all around last Saturday.

Between the hours,
lie, cheat, and steal,
becomes the holy mantra to the soulless husks.

Between the hours,
minds wander to distant lands,
to similar lives where the world's worries disappear.

Between the hours,
happiness clings to the frames,
the ones that hold the faces of those we suffer for.

Pockets

Specks of low lighting are
tucked between bushes.
And in the corners
of carefully placed
drying flowerbeds
are faint stars,
glimmering amongst
the sleepy resort grounds.
Like the Sirens,
the center pool's pump
gurgles in the sea of shadows,
calling out to the Guard who
just began his shift.

Strolling around the midnight grounds,
like a dull coaster fixed upon its straight track,
he wheels himself about,
hitting each checkpoint
logged in a memorized checklist.
Locking the gates and
sweeping the common areas,
he carefully times
the clockwork sprinklers
that burst forth, firing
off like sunken booby traps
in a forbidden throne room.

Soon, he sneaks
to the unattended fridges,
humming lullabies softly.
There, he pockets pilsners,
slugging them back
in the security camera blind spots
and taking in his tiny oasis
as each cool stolen drop
glides along his tongue.
It sparks the sense of freedom
in his forgotten taste buds.
Something the real-world refugees
can afford to feel seasonally.

Please Hold

Conference calls
speak in circles
and bring bad news
to only the blue-collared crew,
leaving the desk dwellers
to hide in dimly lit offices
and stuffy conference rooms.
The poison trickles down
to the masses,
dripping slowly into
the blind eyes
like a punished Loki.
They'll receive
termination notices on telephones
as they are just too afraid
of a face-to-face with reality.
Never witnessing
the strength of decisions
just soaking in
the ink on the paperwork.

Born for the Battle

Dancing around remarks
as if tiptoeing between bear traps.
She draws on a smile
and molds a stiff upper lip.
Anything to keep their sound from drowning out.

Drawn in by dreams,
she shoots for the stars,
only to burn up her wings.
Listening to other familiar soft voices
stuck in their career purgatory,
each whisper about the ways out.
Except for her peers,
the stories fall on sealed ears.
Those ignorant animals have their heads
so low that they scrape the pavement.
So, she stays in the mighty collected,
keeping conversations heated,
and the topic never freezes.
Saving bruised bodies and shells of former selves,
the slaves make more noise
than just rattling chains.

Roars of a proud Valkyrie fly
toward an ever-growing shitstorm.

Women, not on soapboxes but podiums,
take word from hushed corners and craniums
and shove it to the faces at the front.

Strike

Soon he can remove
the plastic seat covers
that are draped along
the backseats of his car
like condoms for the leather.

Soon, he hopes.
Soon he can return to work.
No more shifting eyes
that gaze as if staring
at a horrific car wreck,
the picket line.

Soon…
Soon, he hopes
he won't cater to the cocktails
who stumble from the pubs
after two in the morning.

Soon he won't wander in
at three, exhausted
and thanking God
that he doesn't have to hose
the back seat that night.

Soon, he hopes
there won't be the dreaded
question and answer part of his midday.
So, when his wife and children
ask when the factory
might bust open those gates,
slice that starving line,
and feed the people
back to their stations,
he'll no longer have to answer: soon.

Hurry!

One in the crib;
one in the oven.
Her belly
is the ticking time bomb.
Cupboards are as bare
as both of their wallets.
She pushes,
keeping the wheels going
for the gravy train to keep rolling.
Extra hours here
or missed meals there.
Every bit helps.

Breathing Between the Teeth

Emotions ignite like the flick of a BIC.
A slow burn sizzling in the depths
of my wildfire furnace.
Shriveled thoughts are all that remain
as I bob and weave through the subway.
Just barely holding on,
gripping the filthy silver bar above.
Twitches ravage my face as if
I was defective and flawed.
Released into the public too soon,
now I'm stretched too thin.
The candle burning at both ends
is now the dumpster fire that crackles
in the back of my brain.
I find myself snapping at strangers,
arguing against things I believe
just for a fight.
Just seeking for someone to press
my self-destruction button.
Like the bar flies buzzing
around ice cold pints
or chimneys puffing away
two packs at a time.
Like Atlas, I can physically feel
my world crushing my will beneath the weight.
Packing in more with each stop
the high-speed silver tube makes.

I have less room to breathe.
As the bodies stack around me,
I pant hard like I'm being buried alive.
Pressure rising up, I'm ready to erupt.
Ready to exercise the hell I've carried
all damn day, month, and year.

Steady as She Goes

Another nameless day on the calendar,
but another day, nonetheless.

Knucklehead members,
who could never look in a book,
sit, staring out the window
and praying for escapes
from a town they never embraced.
While Mom is at home
putting her career on hold,
the portion size she prepares
and loads of laundry she washes
continue to grow.
And Dad's running rampant,
dodging layoff letters,
so he's just happy
to stare up at the ceiling
when he finally gets to rest.

Another photo never taken;
another memory developed.

Slow Traffic to the Right

A tomb of twisted metal
doused in the smell of burnt fumes
and the glitter of shattered glass.

The cause of her time loss.
An accident taking the attention
of the nine-to-five commuters.
She sits, scrunched in a line
of flashing break lights.
The multitude of rolling coffins
constructed with hot rubber and demand.
Twelve hours of torment
just to sit and stew
in grievances never spoken,
scolding steam never released.
White knuckles dig into the wheel;
the fire in her gut kept in check,
safe guarded by the seat belt.
The gas tank slowly drains
as the fury builds in her face.
She screams so much that the pain
doesn't follow her home like an abandoned puppy.
Because no one can hear her cries
over car horns and speaker systems.

Motorists might see her on the highway,
but they don't dare get caught
staring at the volcano erupting.

Cut the Check

Imaginary sums are printed on paper.
Ink and envelopes.
Nothing more;
plenty less.

Given value weighing more than bricks.
Collapsing on us.
Covering us;
crushing us.

A shriveling life raft floats in choppy waters.
Keeping heads up.
Holding on;
still kicking.

Steam Whistle

Swimming below the skin's surface,
down in the mental mainframe,
voices bounce back as words replay
and visuals rapidly rewind,
raising the suppressed demons
like a one-man séance.
Fifty whiskey bottles
fill the table space.
Each only holds
the crumb for a mouthful.
Fingers smeared with ink
like fangs dripping fresh blood,
the aftermath of the slaughter
& the emotional decapitation.
Trying to stay ahead
of tomorrow's maze,
while bracing for the impact of today.

Overtime

The barren streets appeared
to stretch on for days,
winding through the empty suburbs.
Traffic lights hadn't tinted
its worn disposition red in
quite some time.
Besides the stars above,
only the scattered Christmas lights twinkled,
blinking from branches
outside neighboring homes.
He zooms along,
uncaring of speed limits
or the little pockets
in the darkened dirt roads
where hidden law enforcement
sit like hunters,
enveloped by night's cover.
He wants to go home
where his wife and daughter
both sleep peacefully,
tucked between warm sheets.

It seems like another lifetime
since he was beside them.
He's off each morning
before their eyelids or the sun could rise.
He returns each night

when they're out like a porch light.
He'll try not to jingle
the doorknob with the key.
Held by his shivering digits.
Like Santa himself,
he can slide in home quietly
and be gone before
the young one awakes.

A few more days
and then he can sleep.
Price tags and long receipts
will all soon be nothing more
than distant worries written in ink.
Every hour, another gift.
Every second worth the work.
And then a new month,
a new year, &
a return to the old schedule.

Too tired to try prepping
for bed ninja silent,
he does it quick
before collapsing to the comfort
that is his bed.
Each night, he hopes
he won't wake his wife.
But like clockwork,
her hands move,

finding his face in the darkness
to bring the stranger in close
for a quick kiss goodnight.

Payday

Storms ceased…
at least for a moment.
Sails capture the cool breeze
that whisks up from the water.
No anchors aboard to weigh us down.
It's smooth sailing from here.

Bodega

Two cats in the kitchen,
and mouse traps by the register where
colorful collections of loosies
sit on display.

One stop shop.

Two trusting employees inside,
husband and wife at opposite ends.
She handles the finances up front,
while he cooks cheap meat at back.

One investment.

Two kids in the back room
upon empty crates and shelves,
pushing pencils to stay good in school.
Forever away from the business.

One family.

Two reasons in their hearts
to endure savage customers of all kinds,
no matter how early lights flicker to life
or how late the door locks tight.

One bodega.

Working Title

Desperate men seeking
work they hate
to better what they love,
despite the cost at their expense.

Hardened backbones
carry the crushing burden
and absorb the gnawing fear,
while daydreaming for the families' sake.

The mourners
crying over the days lost
like they were old ghosts
now earthbound to loom and haunt.

Doomed sons
drown in disease's debt,
fight the new economic debacle
or suffer for their family history.

A man,
broken like a bow,
only knows the limits are
as far as the arrow goes.

About the Author

Chuck is a writer of various forms who currently resides in Los Angeles. He published *Before I Forget* with Black Rose Writing, *What Must Go On* with Unsolicited Press, and *Blooming Insanity* with Dostoyevsky Wannabe.

About the Press

Unsolicited Press is a small publishing house in Portland, Oregon and is dedicated to producing works of fiction, poetry, and nonfiction from a range of voices, but especially the underserved. Our team has published books that aren't afraid to take on topics of race, gender, identity, feminism, patriarchy, mental health, and more. The team is comprised of hardworking volunteers that are passionate about literature.

Learn more at www.unsolicitedpress.com.

www.ingramcontent.com/pod-product-compliance
Lightning Source LLC
Chambersburg PA
CBHW030141100526
44592CB00011B/986